MADONNA

MADONNA

PORTRAIT

OF A

MATERIAL

GIRL

COURAGE
BOOKS

All photos provided by the AGS Picture Archives

Library of Congress Cataloging-in-Publication Number 92-54936

ISBN 1-56138-236-1

Printed and bound in Hong Kong

Cover design by Toby Schmidt
Layout design by Tom Debolski
Captions by Randy Sean Schulman

First published by Courage Books, an imprint of Running Press Book Publishers
125 South Twenty-second Street
Philadelphia, Pennsylvania 19103

contents

the virgin years

*M*adonna. A name that everyone knows, even people who are not Catholic or familiar with Renaissance painting. Madonna the superstar. The singer. The actress. The Boy Toy. The feminist. The filthy-mouthed tramp. The humanist. The multimillionaire bitch. The vixen. The dominatrix. The ubiquitous icon of contemporary culture. That is Madonna.

It began in Michigan in 1958 when the third child of what would become a *large* Catholic family was born and christened Madonna Louise Ciccone. Madonna, or Nonnie, her childhood nickname, led the life of an average middle class girl, participating in school activities that other normal girls do, and having dreams like other normal girls. However, Madonna's dream—to be a star— became her ambition, and she has seen it to fruition.

Madonna left behind a dance scholarship at the University of Michigan and flew to New York a veritable waif. The mythopoeic story has it that she had about $30 when she caught a cab from the airport and demanded to be taken to the center of everything.

Right. Madonna's image changes as quickly as day turns to night. Her obsession with crucifixes was part of an earlier image.

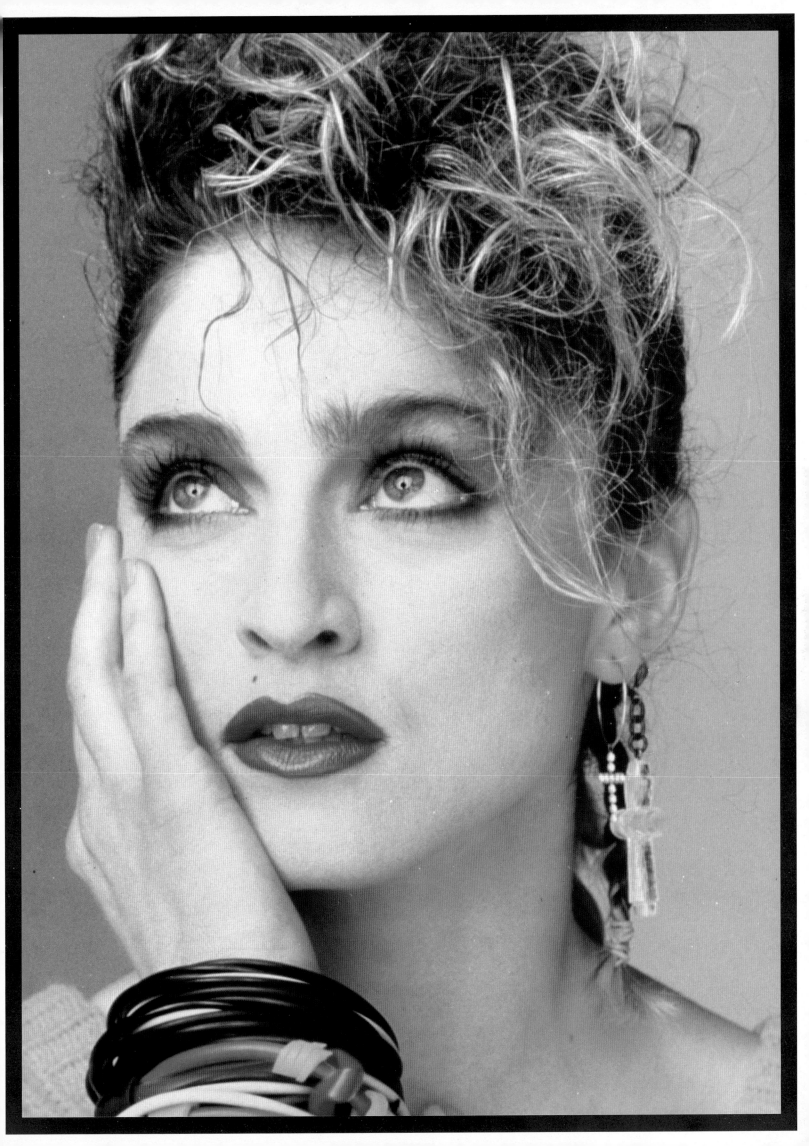

Madonna went from sleeping in the warehouse where her band practiced to living in a fine New York apartment in a matter of months. Her first big break came when Sire Records recorded two singles, "Everybody" and "Borderline," which were played in discotheques and on local radio stations. When these met with approval, Sire offered to make her

first album, *Madonna.* A second album followed, then a hit movie, and doors continued to open for this lucky star.

Judging from the first album, no one could have known what this pop singer would become. Her voice was thin and child-like, her most popular songs were penned by others, and she played an insignificant role on the production end of the album. But fans began to flock to this woman singing what now are Madonna classics like "Holiday," "Lucky Star," "Borderline," "Physical Attraction," and "Everybody."

It was not all luck, however. Madonna achieved her life-long dream because she is intelligent and ambitious. The combination of opportunity and hard work, has brought this woman to the level of popularity she now enjoys. The woman has a compulsive personality, and she is never dormant. An example of the sense for business Madonna has had from the very beginning, the first expensive thing she bought when she started making some money was a Roland synthesizer, putting the profits back into the business. (The other items she purchased with her new-found wealth were lacy lingerie.)

Right: Madonna sporting a simple hat, red parasol, T-shirt, and an anything-but-flashy jacket. The glamour still shines through.

Below: Stretching her talents, ambitions, flash-in-the-pan images, hopes and dreams, over and around all boundaries, helped her reach the very top—a place she plans to stay.

Left: Who's that girl who dared to wear purple lipstick? Madonna, that's who. Fashion statements have long been a part of her focus on success. Starting trends seems just as important to Madonna as her music career.

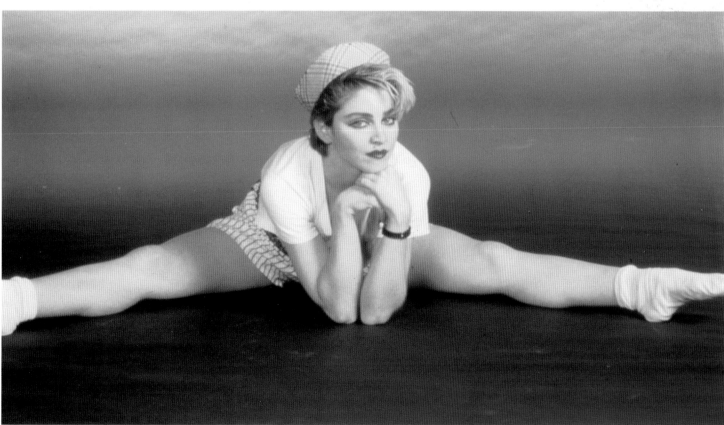

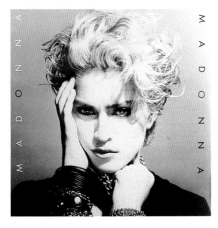

For the first few months of Madonna's arriving on the scene of pop music, she was just a voice. Many people assumed she was African American. In fact, her songs were aired primarily on black radio stations for the first few months. It was not until the release of the video "Burning Up" in the middle of 1983 that fans saw the face (and body) that the voice belonged to. Needless to say, they were pleased.

The image Madonna created was startling and unusual, downright strange at the time. This would be just the first look of Madonna's ever-changing persona. The black bra was something worn on the inside until the Madonna revolution. She set one fashion trend after another, making

At top: Madonna, as sultry as ever on the cover of her debut album—*Madonna* (1983).
Out of it came her smash hit "Borderline," just one of her top 10 singles.

Above: Her true colors come through in this early photo. Red, purple, black, blue, green, and yellow are only a part of the colorful character she emanates.

Right: The icon always appears poised and comfortable in front of an audience. She develops a rapport with her fans and gives them exactly what they want.

the black bra an essential part of every hip woman's wardrobe, along with the O-ring bracelets, which were actually typewriter drive belts, and the dangling crucifixes. The original Madonna look consisted of mismatched layers of clothes, hose and rags tied in her hair, myriad black rubber bracelets on her wrists and up her arms, and crucifixes hanging around her neck and dangling from her ears, as well as other appendages. Other components were the fingerless gloves, netting, and ankle-high boots. But while Madonna fans across the nation and throughout the world were donning these accoutrements, Madonna was creating another look. In fact, a key to her growing popularity was the intrigue she created with each image she projected. And she never gave her look a chance to get old, fascinating people both male and female.

Above: Sex appeal seems to come naturally to the musical superstar. Even in this early photo she expresses a sensuality rare to many pop artists. The sexy, controversial image of the 1980s helped her skyrocket to success. Today? Madonna is still the subject of controversy, but her sexuality has given birth to a goddess.

She was setting a massive fashion trend which had retailers scrambling to manufacture official "Boy Toy" clothing and jewelry. Some department stores had "Madonna" sections featuring the raggedy clothes and make-shift bracelets, and they held Madonna look-alike contests.

Madonna's national television debut was on January 14, 1984. She appeared on American Bandstand lip-synching to her hit "Holiday." It was then that Madonna informed Dick Clark of her ambition: to rule the world.

Though many people don't realize it, Madonna's first movie was *Vision Quest,* but her role was small. Yet she was the high point of an otherwise unmemorable movie about a high school wrestler on his journey of initiation. She played herself, singing "Crazy For You" and "Gambler" in a nightclub.

Soon, people would get a more intimate look at the singer as she turned actress with a role in *Desperately Seeking Susan.* Playing the title character, Madonna essentially plays herself, even wearing her characteristic attire, which really cemented the look. She was virtually unknown when she was picked for the role, but by the time the movie was ready for release, Madonna was hot. The movie originally was supposed to have an ensemble cast, but when it was released, Madonna was on the charts with "Like A Virgin," so the film inevitably became hers. Ultimately Madonna upstaged the intended star of the movie, Rosanna Arquette.

In *Desperately Seeking Susan,* Madonna plays a character much like herself, a free-spirited, unusual, clever woman who says and does what she wants. Madonna admitted that the character was very similar to her own. The only difference, according to her, is that the real woman has goals and direction. Susan is floating through life in limbo.

The film is a light-hearted comedy incorporating the classic formula of amnesia, mistaken identity, and an ancient valuable artifact. It is very much a women's production, with the writer, producer, director, and stars all female. The success of this film must be partly attributable to the camaraderie and sisterhood depicted in this film. Arquette plays a bored

At top: Madonna entices the crowd by crooning one of her many hits.

Above: It all started with black bracelets and cool hair. But it's the kiss that may contain the secret of her success.

Far left: The eyes alone can tell a story. Mystery, intrigue, determination, talent, strong will, and a good head for business are just a few qualities that can take a girl from Bay City, Michigan, and propel her to universal stardom.

housewife who fantasizes about the lives of two lovers who communicate through classified ads in the personal section. When this character gets amnesia, she thinks she is Susan, and a comedy of errors unfolds.

The second album, *Like A Virgin,* followed a year later, long before the enthusiasm for the first died out. On this album, Madonna exercised more control over the production aspect and wrote six of the songs herself. Hits from this recording include "Material Girl," "Love Don't Live Here Any-more," "Dress You Up," and, of course, "Like A Virgin." The album *Like a Virgin* was released in November of 1984, and by January it was number one on the charts.

But before the album was released, Madonna debuted the title song, "Like A Virgin," on the MTV awards. This performance launched a steady frigate of controversy that would follow and help bolster Madonna's

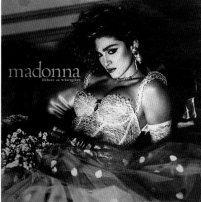

Above: Madonna's second album, *Like A Virgin*, was released in 1984, giving rise to one of her biggest singles, "Like A Virgin." This young performer was no longer a virgin to the music industry.

Right: Madonna as Susan with costar Rosanna Arquette, who played Roberta in *Desperately Seeking Susan*. Roberta is a housewife who loses her identity and thinks she is Susan.

popularity throughout her career. She strutted across and humped the stage belting her new song, as cameramen slinked around getting compromising vantage points of the unsuspecting performer. The viewing audience got a peek at Madonna's garters and more.

Madonna did not rest on the laurels of this popular album and the hit movie *Desperately Seeking Susan,* however. She moved on to her next project, making the videos.

The title song's video was filmed in Madonna's homeland of Italy, in Venice, and she co-stars with a lion-man. In the video, Madonna writhes around on a long, sleek, phallic gondola, paces across a room in a gorgeous, traditional wedding dress with an abundant train, and stares

meditatively through a multi-layered veil. Likewise, a lion paces expectantly across a columned corridor. Finally the bride is gathered up by the lion, who now has the body of a man, and is laid down on the wedding bed, but the viewer can only imagine how the consummation went; that is the end of the video.

Expectantly, the religious right condemned as blasphemous the song, the video, and this tart who calls herself by the name of the mother of God. Little did they know that this was mild compared to what Madonna had in store.

The "Material Girl" video initiated Madonna's Marilyn Monroe image. Its motif is the "Diamonds Are a Girl's Best Friend" scene from the classic

Monroe film *Gentlemen Prefer Blondes,* and Madonna emulates Monroe to a tee. She even wears a dress identical to Monroe's in the classic movie. Madonna dances among a group of enamored suitors, casting off the ones who fail to offer her the right kind of gifts. One rejected lover goes tumbling down the flight of stairs they are dancing on, and Madonna saunters down and hikes her high-heeled foot up on his chest in the stance of victory. Meanwhile, a rich filmmaker has the hots for the starlet and engages in a behind-the-scenes pursuit to win her heart. Discovering that the actress is really not a material girl, the suitor disguises himself as an average Joe, and the down-to-earth woman who likes a blue-collar kind of guy is fooled into falling for a material boy.

While filming this video, Madonna met her future husband, Sean Penn. She happened to have an extra rose after giving roses to the cast and crew, and she presented Sean with it.

Far left: On the set of *Desperately Seeking Susan:* The hat. The glasses. The dangling cigarette. It's all a part of Madonna's cool, character, and charisma.

Below: Madonna the singer, the actress,... and the film director? It hasn't happened yet, but don't put it past this creatively ambitious performer.

The pair began dating immediately. Sean was an established member of the Hollywood community, more specifically the Brat Pack (including Timothy Hutton, Emilio Estevez, Tom Cruise, Rob Lowe, and Judd Nelson), since his mother was an actor and his father a director. So he took Madonna to parties given by stars, where she met two more people who would play prominent roles in her life, Warren Beatty and Sandra Bernhard. The couple also visited Marilyn Monroe's grave.

Not long after Madonna and Sean began their relationship, reports of Sean's temper and intolerance of the press made headlines. But Madonna was convinced that he was the perfect American man, (she thought he resembled her father), and she accepted his marriage proposal in Nashville while he was filming At Close Range. Penn was Madonna's hero and best friend. A few days after the proposal, Penn's assault on a photographer spawned a million dollar lawsuit.

Nineteen-eighty-five was becoming a busy year for Madonna. The "Material Girl" video was released on February 1 and Vision Quest on February 15. Desperately Seeking Susan was released on March 29 and was accompanied by the "Into the Groove" video. During the first half of the year, there were five current videos in rotation on MTV and six singles on the charts. Early that year, Like A Virgin went triple platinum, and her first album was still on the charts. Like A Virgin eventually

sold over 4.5 million copies in the United States and 2.5 million abroad. She had taken the world by storm.

Madonna was the most visible woman in the universe. She had hit songs and videos, and two films. Her image was on the cover of magazines all over the world. In 1985, *People* alone featured her on the cover four times. As if this were not enough, Madonna launched a concert tour.

The Virgin Tour provided an opportunity for thousands of fans to see the multimedia blitzing star in the flesh. It was an energetic show featur-

Above: Madonna and friend Rosanna Arquette backstage of the July 13, 1985 Live-Aid concert at Philadelphia's JFK Stadium. The concert, a fundraiser to fight famine in Ethiopia, was broadcast live by satellite from JFK Stadium and Wembley Stadium in London to more than one billion people around the world.

ing the songs from her first two albums. The then-unknown rap band Beastie Boys opened the show which ran from April 10 to June 8, 1985, and spanned the country.

The night she played in Detroit, her hometown, during "Holiday" she yelled, "There's no place like home," and after a few moments of fighting back tears said, "You know, I was never elected the homecoming queen or anything, but I sure feel like one now!"

Beginning the show with "Dress You Up," Madonna wore a multi-colored leather jacket over a blue diaphanous blouse, purple tights, clinging blue skirt, high-top boots, and crucifixes to spare. Most of her outfits had cut-out or embroidered crosses in them. The real fashion statement was made with the cropped wedding dress that she wore for "Like A Virgin." It had all the makings of a traditional wedding dress except for a mid-section. For "Material Girl," Madonna lost the lace skirt and gained a white fur stole. Her male dancers offered her money for her affections, which she grabbed and stuffed down her blouse. When that was not enough, she skipped around picking the pockets of her band members. Finally, she proclaimed that she is not really a material girl, that she doesn't need money, she just needs love. Then her scolding father whisked her off the stage as though she were a naughty child.

Above: Taking fashion to new heights is part of her intrigue, including Madonna's version of a wedding dress. Donning this outfit, she concluded every *Virgin* tour in (1984) with an encore of "Like A Virgin."

Far left: A look once thought of as virtuous—now sexy, hot, and alluring. One of Madonna's many looks as she seduces her fans in a white lace outfit.

Although 1985 was a splendid year for the ambitious entertainer, not all would go her way. The September issues of *Penthouse* and *Playboy* magazines would feature nude photos of Madonna that were taken

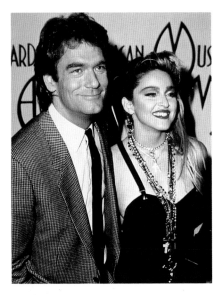

years before when she was a model for artists. This was one of the few times when Madonna did not have utter control over the direction of her career, and that was the upsetting part for her, but negative press has failed to thwart Madonna every time; it just propels her popularity.

In fact, the photographs are in no way prurient or exploitative. They are beautiful black and white nudes by photographers Lee Friedlander and Martin Schreiber. The integrity in question was not that of Madonna for posing but of these photographers, who obviously wanted to cash in on someone else's success. Soon after the nude photo scandal, Madonna performed at the Live Aid concert where she proclaimed, "I ain't taking shit off today! You might hold it against me in five years," pointing to the vindictiveness of the people who sold the photos. *Playboy* showed its pornographic side when Madonna refused $1 million to pose nude by

sending advanced copies of their Madonna issue to Sean Penn.

Another opportunist cashing in on the success of Madonna was Stephen Lewicki who released *A Certain Sacrifice,* an amateurish Super-8 film he had made starring Madonna before she became famous. In this bizarre film, Madonna's character, Bruna, is the dominatrix in a family of lovers, which are like creepy earth dwellers.

The primary reason Madonna attempted to stop the release of this video is the fact that Bruna is not a good character for Madonna to play. She is a victim from beginning to end. There is no growth.

It seemed as though Madonna's past were coming back to haunt her, yet she remained unscathed.

The most famous wedding since Charles and Di's occurred on August 16, 1985, coincidentally Madonna's birthday. Madonna and Sean tied one on for the tying of the knot. The gala event took place at the edge of a cliff at a $6 million Malibu mansion belonging to a friend of the Penn family. Madonna admits that the wedding had a circus atmosphere with 13 helicopters hovering overhead during the ceremony, Sean trying to punch out a cameraman, and Madonna and Sean clowning with the wedding cake smearing tradition. Madonna dressed up in a real wedding dress this time, a traditional one to boot.

Three months later, on Saturday Night Live, Madonna lampooned the event with a hilarious mock-video in which she shoots down the helicopters with an uzi.

Above: All smiles from the woman on the road to fame and fortune. After the American Music Awards in the mid-1980s, Madonna's career progressed to levels she could never have imagined. Or could she?

Top left: Madonna and Huey Lewis at the American Music Awards.

Far left: The gossip hounds loved this dynamic duo. Sean Penn hated the paparazzi, which contributed to the couples' problems from their dating days, through their marriage on August 16, 1985, and eventually their divorce three years later.

who's that girl?

n o rest for the honeymooner, however. Madonna began work on her third album *True Blue,* which was released in 1986. This time Madonna exercised even more control over production and co-wrote all the songs except for "Papa Don't Preach," written by Brian Elliot, with Madonna taking credit for additional lyrics. Two songs on this compilation pay respect to famous rebels: "White Heat" is dedicated to actor James Cagney for his film of the same name, as she pays tribute to the 1930's gangster movies; and "Jimmy Jimmy," honors actor James Dean. With "Love Makes the World Go Round," Madonna pays another kind of tribute to the peace songs of the 1960s. The ballad "Live to Tell" served as the theme song of Sean's movie *At Close Range.* Other hits from this release are "La Isle Bonita," "Where's the Party," "Open Your Heart," and the title song "True Blue." The *True Blue* album was the most expressive and personal to date. Both "Papa Don't Preach" and *True Blue* were number one on the charts by August 1986.

With *True Blue,* Madonna presented a new image of herself. Gone were the jewelry and matted, rag-tied hairdo. The new Madonna was stripped

Far right. Madonna sports short hair during her *True Blue* era in 1986. By this time she had more power in the decision-making aspect of her songs, concerts, and videos, than in the past.

down, sporting cropped blonde hair, short, 1950s-style capri pants, sleek, form-fitting tops, and no jewelry. Madonna called this unadorned look feminine and glamorous. This was the antithesis to the original Madonna look, and the fans loved it.

The most talked about video from *True Blue* was "Papa Don't Preach," which portrays a girl's relationship with her father. This video was the first to visually tell a story to go along with the lyrics. Madonna appears as a pregnant teenager who is determined to stay with her boyfriend and have their baby. The conflict arises when the single parent, a blue-collar man who has raised the girl by himself, cannot come to terms with his daughter's decision. An adult, sleek, platinum blonde Madonna sings the lyrics and dances in a black strapless, figure-revealing outfit. She is the narrator of the girl's monologue.

Above and opposite, top: Madonna always sings from the heart. Her beauty transfixes an audience, her voice holds them in her palms, and her power and energy never lets them go. Take away the jewelry, long hair, and fancy clothes, and you still get a dazzling, sexy, energetic, and powerful performer. After all, she's Madonna.

This song and video were not without controversy. The pro-lifers finally had a reason to like Madonna. More importantly, though, many people believed that the video romanticized teenage pregnancy, misleading impressionable teenage girls. Little recognition goes to the singer, who donated a considerable percentage of the profits from this song to programs that promoted sexual responsibility.

Also from her latest album came the single "Open Your Heart," a song which asserts woman's command over the sexual realm, which Madonna says is a little scary for both women and men. This song became the third number one hit from this album. The video for it was met with some expected controversy. Madonna plays an exotic dancer in a peep show. This is a sexual video, including homosexual and androgynous images. A young boy wants to get in the show to see the performer pictured in a poster hanging by the ticket window. The old ticket-taker will not give in, so the boy stands outside, fantasizing about the nude women on the posters. Inside, the dancer performs in a black teddy with torpedo-shaped breasts that have gold sequins and black tassels. She is encircled by windows through which her customers view her. The clients consist of homosexual sailors, horny old buzzards, and a giggling young man. Madonna is the dancer who does not pay attention to her viewers. Suddenly, the dancer appears outside, cross-dressed in a grey suit matching that of the kid. She kisses the young fantasizer on the lips and the two dance away together, leaving the old ticket-taker in a tizzy. (Coincidentally, the actor who plays the boy, Chris Finch, also went on tour with Madonna.)

Madonna had less success with her next film venture—*Shanghai Surprise*—in which she co-starred with Sean. (She and her husband also worked together on an experimental theater production called *Goose*

Above and left: True Blue, Madonna's third album, assured her center stage for a long time to come. The hit single and video, *Papa Don't Preach* earned her an MTV Music Video Award for Best Female Video in 1987. Madonna dedicated *True Blue* to Sean—'the coolest guy in the universe." Apparently, being cool wasn't enough reason for the two being together.

and *Tomtom,* which failed to take off as well.) In *Shanghai Surprise* Madonna portrays a missionary who breaks the feminine mold of the 1930s by volunteering overseas. Her character, Gloria Tatlock, is a missionary who aids a crook, played by Penn, in locating a shipment of opium.

Madonna was attracted to the role because the character is a strong individual who is adventurous and does not succumb to the pressure on women to stay home and raise families. Another factor in her decision to take the part had to do with her critics, who claimed that the only reason Madonna was a success in *Desperately Seeking Susan* was because she played herself. Madonna wanted to prove her acting abilities by playing a completely opposite character. It was obvious, however, that at this point in her career people loved this woman for being herself, not someone's fictional character. When *Shanghai Surprise* was released in August, it met with dismal reviews and low ticket sales.

Towards the end of 1986 Madonna began work on a new movie called *Slammer,* which would become *Who's That Girl.* Madonna did not have to steal the show this time; this movie was all hers. She played a character named Nikki Finn who sets out to clear her name from a murder rap after she is released from prison. The reception of this effort, though bet-

Above: Madonna's third movie, *Shanghai Surprise* (1986) was a box office flop. She played Gloria, a young woman who left her home in Massachusetts to do missionary work. She falls for a smooth-talking character played by Sean Penn. The director was shooting for a chemistry similar to that of Humphrey Bogart and Katharine Hepburn in *The African Queen.*

Right: If at first you don't succeed, try, try again. *Who's That Girl?* (1987) Madonna's fourth motion picture, was another failure. She played Nikki Finn, a woman jailed for a crime she didn't commit. Her methods for trying to set the record straight get her into more trouble.

ter than *Shanghai Surprise*, was still not good. When *Who's That Girl* premiered on August 6, 1987, the reviews were unfavorable. Madonna still had not successfully melded singing and acting, but she was determined; Judy Garland did it!

Madonna hit the road again in mid-1987 with the *Who's That Girl Tour*. This second concert was more spectacular, like a stage show. Thought-provoking images were projected on a huge screen behind the stage to accompany the songs and dancing. Among various images, including those of authority figures, flashed "SAFE SEX," revealing Madonna's concern for the growing number of people contracting AIDS. Madonna believes that with her fame comes the responsibility to be a spokesperson, and her messages are positive and affirming. Tickets were sold out for every show, which travelled to eighteen cities and three continents, and each concert grossed about $500,000.

In the vein of earnings, in 1987 *Forbes* magazine rated Madonna among the top earning entertainers, with a gross income of $26 million.

In November 1987, Madonna released a dance compilation called *You Can Dance*, which is a line from "Into the Groove" that had become a credo. The recording features her most popular danceable songs remixed to perfection by the hottest DJs. Madonna's old boyfriend Jellybean Benitez reworked "Holiday," and Shep Pettibone mixed "Into the

Below: Madonna tried to prove herself as a serious actress in *Shanghai Surprise*. But critics didn't respond as she'd hoped. Still, you have to give the singer-turned-actress credit for taking on new challenges—something Madonna lives for. Nobody's infallible—not even this beauty queen.

Groove" and "Where's the Party" for this special release. Other re-releases are "Spotlight," "Physical Attraction," and "Over and Over."

By the end of 1987, Madonna was working on *Bloodhounds of Broadway* with Jennifer Grey, Randy Quaid, and Matt Dillon. She plays Hortense Hathaway, a 1920s nightclub showgirl. This film was produced for PBS's American Playhouse but ultimately was only released on video for lack of sponsorship.

Behind the scenes of Madonna's public life during 1986 and 1987, she lost friends to AIDS, a loss which fueled her efforts to raise money for AIDS research. She participated in benefits and donated the proceeds

from her New York *Who's That Girl Tour* show at Madison Square Garden. Madonna has lost close friends Christopher Flynn, Martin Burgoyne, Keith Haring, and Andy Warhol to this disease. She has donated close to a million dollars to AIDS research and participated in fund-raising efforts. Not stopping there, she passes out information sheets on AIDS to her audiences at concerts and to fans who buy her music. She knows and is compassionate to her audience, taking some responsibility for their well-being.

Madonna continued striving to conquer the realm of acting. In 1988, she appeared in what originally was intended to be an off-broadway production called *Speed-the-Plow*. The superstar's popularity won the play a spot on broadway before it even

Above: Just a few of the people who fussed over Madonna during the filming of *Who's That Girl?* A petite woman surrounded by big people, structures, and publicity. And she loves every minute of it.

Right: Feet Samuels (Randy Quaid) and Hortense Hathaway (Madonna), in 1989s *Bloodhounds of Broadway*. Feet is ready to do everything he can to win the love of Hortense.

Far left: The finest champagne for one of the world's finest performers.

opened. The play, written by Pulitzer Prize winner David Mamet, whose work Madonna admires, is a diatribe on Hollywood, examining the conflict between art and commercialism.

Madonna played Karen, a temporary secretary at a film production company who tries to influence a film producer to back a project that has more integrity. Again, Madonna was attracted to this role by the character, who at the start of the play is a victim but by the end has become more powerful.

Though every show sold out, reviews were mixed about Madonna's abilities as an actress. She herself grew to resent the monotony of performing the same thing every night; she began feeling caged in.

Around this time, as her marriage with Sean withered, Madonna was developing a new friendship with Sandra Bernhard, who also had a show on Broadway, *Without You I'm Nothing*. The marriage to Penn ended with the year, yet Madonna maintained in her documentary *Truth or Dare* that Sean remains the love of her life.

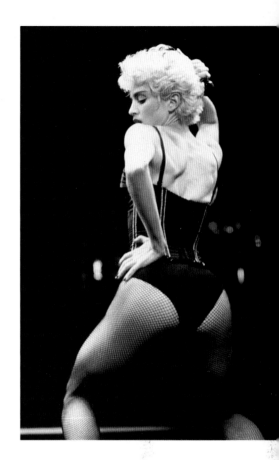

Above: Madonna promises a hot and spicy performance. Whether she's having a bad or good day, she always comes through in the end.

Left: She's crooned her way into fans" hearts all around the world. Madonna was surrounded by fancy sets, lighting, and costumes during the opening of the *Who's That Girl* concert. But the audience was transfixed by the superstar. It is the woman they find most appealing—for she appeals to a great variety of people.

Far left: A pointy bustier and a six-shooter to boot. Madonna's a quick draw for creating new images to keep her fans guessing. Is it the hat that throws you off?

breath-less

*a*fter a three-year hiatus, Madonna was back in the recording studio, and in 1988 she released an album that revealed her growth as an individual.

Like A Prayer was something totally new for Madonna. It brought a new sound and a new look. This was Madonna's best release ever. The songs were all written by her, and they revealed the most personal, truthful side of Madonna that the world had ever seen. The lyrics on *Like A Prayer* are semi-autobiographical with "Till Death Do Us Part" addressing her marriage, "Oh Father" commenting on the dual authority of her father and the church, and "Keep It Together," a message to her siblings.

The album was not only sound but sight and smell as well. Every jacket got a splash of patchouli oil, and on the cover was a photo of Madonna from the thighs to just above the belly-button, in hip-hugger jeans reminiscent of the 1960s.

The sound is oriented in the 1960's music style as well, and Madonna's voice had deepened and gotten fuller. The album deals with complex, mature themes. Unlike the light-hearted pop songs of the past, these

Right: She takes your breath away. Madonna plays Breathless Mahoney in the 1990 much-anticipated film *Dick Tracy*. Her performance was well-received and she set the silver screen ablaze with her fiery sensuality.

semi-autobiographical pieces are full of emotion and substance. No one had seen this side of Madonna before. This time, critics were taking the woman seriously as a singer and an artist. Madonna finally received the recognition and respect that she was after from her critics. People who never thought they would, considered Madonna as an entertainer of integrity.

Pepsi advanced Madonna $5 million to endorse their cola just before the album was released. They created the first commercial featuring the adult Madonna and an actor portraying Madonna as a young girl. The little girl sees what she will become, and the adult Madonna steps into the past, seeing where she has come from. At the end, the adult

Above: Madonna's fourth album was 1989s *Like A Prayer* in which sexual and religious symbols played a big part of the theme. It sparked one of her most controversial moments of being in the spotlight when church leaders decided that the *Like A Prayer* video was blasphemous. The song, however, stayed at the number one spot on the charts for over a month.

Right: What could this possibly mean? Maybe nothing. The point is that Madonna makes you think. Standing in front of a men's urinal may not be her most glamorous photo, but it's intriguing to say the least.

Far right: Didn't James Dean strike a pose like this? Maybe it's just the cool eyes and cigarette effect. Although James Dean wouldn't have worn lipstick—in public anyway. Still, it seems that Madonna enjoys playing around with the looks of 1950s icons.

Madonna says "Make A Wish" and they both drink Pepsi. The day after this sweet commercial was aired, Madonna's "Like A Prayer" video debuted on MTV. The images in the video are nothing like the sentimental commercial, and the religious right, led by the American Family Association, had a fit.

Pepsi buckled under the pressure from various religious sects and in cowardly style pulled the ad and cancelled the deal with Madonna. She got to keep the advance, though.

The "Like A Prayer" video oscillates between spiritual and carnal ecstasy, showing burning crucifixes, Madonna being very sexual in a church, and stigmata on her hands as though she had been crucified. That was all that was needed to start a holy war.

The video is an intriguing compilation of imagery. There is a duality in story. The realistic side involves Madonna's persona witnessing an injustice, the arrest of a black man for molesting and murdering a woman, a crime that was actually committed by a white man. Meanwhile, the persona seeks refuge in an African American church where events become symbolic rather than actual. Madonna is beckoned to this church as if she were chosen to set things straight. In the church, she liberates a crying icon and dances with a gospel choir. She interacts a large part of the time with one woman from the choir who also symbolically lifts her soul up when it has fallen. Interspersed are scenes of Madonna dancing and singing among a group of burning crosses. The interpretations that can be drawn from these scenes are numerous, and for many religious leaders, sacrilege came to mind. But when one considers the whole video and not just certain scenes, the burning crosses represent injustice and the burning desire for spiritual truth.

The "Express Yourself" video, costing $1 million, was the most expensive rock video produced to date. This video gained notoriety with its images of sadomasochism. There is a dichotomy between the harsh industrial underworld where muscular men flex their muscles on heavy machinery and the "higher ground" represented by Madonna's elegant persona in 1950's-era glamorous gowns in an art deco environment. The cat exists in both realms and is the unifying link. As the gears churn below, above the woman sings affirming words about love, that a woman is better off on her own than compromising in her choice of a partner. The relationship has to be based on intellectual, not just sexual compatibility. The woman then dances powerfully in a man's suit bearing her black bra and grabbing her crotch. She is a powerful, independent image. Next she is prone on a bed bound in an iron collar at the end of a long chain, suggesting a sadomasochistic sort of submission. So the images are indeterminant. Eventually a man from the depths comes up to where the woman is, as if he has learned to balance his masculine and feminine sides as she has done, and there is harmony. "With-

Above: Expressing herself comes naturally for Madonna. With her *Express Yourself* video in 1989, she makes that poignantly clear.

Right: Milky white skin gives Madonna an irresistibly edible quality even her *Express Yourself* co-star can't ignore.

Far right: It isn't too often that Madonna appears vulnerable. Shackles and chains just about does it. However, this is a scene out of *Express Yourself*, not her real life. You don't think Madonna would really do things like that—do you?

out the heart/ there can be/ no understanding/ between the hand/ and the mind" appears on the screen at the video's end.

"Cherish" was visually interpreted by photographer Herb Ritts and shows Madonna frolicking on the beach with a Boy-fish. The result is aesthetically lush; in black and white, Madonna is seen playing in the surf while a trio of Man-fish glide whale-like through the sea.

"Oh Father" is a beautiful video in which the lyrics and the images stay aligned. The father referred to in the title is not only the persona's parent but also the priest, or rather the Catholic church. The song tells about a woman who was hurt by her father and as a result has gotten away from him. The video embellishes this emancipation theme. It depicts the death of a young girl's mother and the little girl frolicking oblivious to the loss, and playing in the attic with her mother's jewels. Her father catches her and scolds her. The little girl looks at her mother in the casket and sees that her lips have been sewn together. As an adult, the woman discovers that she is in the same abusive environment with her lover as she was with her father. The lyrics apply to both men as well. She leaves her lover, with the understanding that he is that way because someone hurt him too. Then she appears in a confessional repeating the same words along with saying she has sinned. The question of what her sin was is not answered. She has the guilt without having deserved it. The guilt was put on her by the father figures in her life. There are images of the little girl

jumping trying to reach the handle of a door while menacing large shadows cross over her. Finally there is some sort of resolution between the father and adult daughter as they stand at the grave. The final vision is of the little girl dancing on her mother's grave. the persona is a strong woman who has escaped the inhibiting confining lifestyle, saying, "You can't hurt me now. I got away from you. I never thought I would. You can't make me cry. You once had the power. I never felt so good about myself." She is triumphant, but the victory is tinged with sadness and loss.

The song is beautifully done with slide guitars and cherubic harmony.

The video is done in crisp black and white, and the images are rich and multilayered. Madonna is strong and beautiful in this personal autobiographical work.

Madonna has admitted that she has a mother complex. Since her mother died of breast cancer when she was six, Madonna has always felt

a void. Growing up without her mother has made her crave the love and attention of the world. It has also forced her to deal with her own mortality, knowing that her chances of getting the same disease are high.

Meanwhile Madonna continued supporting various causes with her participation in an AIDS benefit dance-athon and a concert to benefit the salvation of the rain forest, in which she co-starred with Sandra Bernhard, both dressed in retro-hippie hip-huggers and bare mid-riff blouses. Together they performed their rendition of Sonny and Cher's "I Got You Babe," ad-libbing some of the lyrics to cause a stir.

Dick Tracy was released in June 1990. Finally Madonna had achieved success as an actress. She played the chanteuse cartoon character Breathless Mahoney. Madonna so desired this role that she settled for union scale wages, $1,440 a week, although she negotiated for a percentage of the royalties. But she got the honor of starring in a film with the likes of Warren Beatty, Al Pachino, and Dustin Hoffman. Besides working with such distinguished actors, Madonna felt drawn to the character of Breathless because she is a seductress in a lot of pain and

Above: Madonna on the beach in her *Cherish* video. She didn't make waves with this one—just got soaked and played in the sand.

Far right: Madonna and co-star of *Dick Tracy*, Warren Beatty, sizzled on screen and off. But the off-screen romance fizzled in only a few months.

someone who has never been loved. Can Madonna relate?

In *Dick Tracy*, Madonna, as the victimized seductress Breathless Mahoney, who is a cross between Marilyn Monroe and Jessica Rabbit, always wearing a décolleté gown and a hand on her hip, works as a chanteuse for Big Boy (Al Pachino) the gangster/owner of a nightclub. On the surface, Breathless is a sad woman who cannot win the heart of *Dick Tracy*, whom she has fallen in love with because he is the first person to treat her with respect. But there turns out to be more to this beautiful face than anyone expects.

In this comic-strip film with its unreal color and cartoon characters, Madonna sings songs by Stephen Sondheim and Andy Paley that emulate the 1930's era. The songs were the toughest challenge for the pop singer to master, but with the assistance of a vocal coach, Madonna gives an impressive performance.

Besides union wages, Madonna had to put up with Beatty's perfectionism, shooting multiple takes of scenes until they were absolutely perfect. This had to be difficult for an actress who always thought the first take was her best.

An offshoot of *Dick Tracy* was the short-lived romance between Madonna and Warren Beatty. Madonna likes men who are in touch with both

At top: Madonna and Warren taking care of business—the business of seduction.

Above: "I'm Breathless," a 1990 release was inspired by the film *Dick Tracy*. It features "Sooner or Later," "Now I'm Following You," and "Hanky Panky'—three songs that introduce a different Madonna with a different way of singing. It evokes the times of torch songs and swing tunes.

Far right: Try not to look too deep into her eyes. There's a spell somewhere in there that has a profound effect on those who dare. Isn't it the truth?

their masculine and feminine sides, and that was the appealing feature of Warren. (The public gets a rare peek at the couple interacting behind the scenes in her documentary.)

Attending the Academy Awards with her surprise date, Michael Jackson, Madonna performed "Sooner or Later (I Always Get My Man)" from the movie, wearing $20 million-worth of borrowed diamonds and vamping her heart out in a sparkling 1930s-style Bob Mackie gown and an ermine stole. "Sooner or Later" won the Best Original Song award.

Madonna released *I'm Breathless,* a recording of the songs she did for the film and ones that were inspired by the era of *Dick Tracy,* including

"Vogue," which became Madonna's eighth number one single. This hit is a summons to all to be glamorous. The video for the song features Madonna "voguing," which is much like posing, in a see-through black lace blouse.

The album *I'm Breathless* features three Sondheim songs, "Sooner or Later," "More," and "What Can You Lose" and two by Paley, "Now I'm Following You" and "I'm Going Bananas." The others are Madonna's own, which she co-wrote mostly with Patrick Leonard, "He's a Man," "Hanky Panky," "Cry Baby," "Something To Remember," "Back in Business," and "I'm Following You (Part II)." "Vogue" she co-wrote with Shep Pettibone.

In May 1990 Madonna launched her unforgettable *Blond Ambition Tour*. This show encapsulated all of Madonna the Performer, singing, dancing, and acting. She was in the best shape of her life both physically and vocally. The *Blond Ambition Tour* kicked off in Tokyo on April 13, 1990, and the shows were always sold out.

Having loads of experience touring by this time, Madonna was determined to make this show interesting for *herself* as well as the audience. Madonna sees this show as an emotional journey dealing with woman's role in society. It began aggressive and hostile, journeyed through worship and adoration, tried to merge sexual and religious passion, cast out

Above: Breathless Mahoney as Madonna, or Madonna as Breathless? Both characters radiate a sophisticated and captivating sex appeal, much like the glamour girls of an earlier era.

Right: Madonna kicked off her *Blonde Ambition* tour on April 13, 1990 in Chiba, Japan.

male authority figures, ran away, and then ended on a note of unity and familial piety. The artist changed roles, showing woman as protagonist and man in peripheral roles. All of this was done through a humorous vein, leaving the intent ambiguous.

In a gender-bending pin-striped suit, with slits at the breasts that reveal a dangerous looking bra, a corset on the outside of the pants, and with a foot-long blond I-Dream-of-Jeannie ponytail, Madonna began her theatrical production with a crotch-grabbing rendition of "Express Yourself." The set was of an industrial metropolis emulating the one from the video. That went straight into "Open Your Heart," which had a similar chair routine as the video, but instead of the young

Above: Madonna's music, mixed with a bit of performance art, added to the uniqueness of the *Blonde Ambition* tour. She was now trying to create a new image for concerts—she succeeded.

Far right: The multitalented Madonna gracefully playing the harp during the *Ambition* tour.

boy, Madonna danced with Oliver, one of her dancers. Then, zipping into a striped boxing blouse, Madonna and her singers, Niki Harris and Donna Delory, had a boxing match to "Causing a Commotion," which resulted in Madonna's utter victory. "Where's the Party" got the singers back into a friendly mood, as the gears churned in the background.

The scene changed to that of a bedroom through the skillful use of hydraulics, and a red bed rose to center stage from below with the corseted diva in the center. Slow, intriguing oriental music played as she sang a slowed-down version of "Like A Virgin," while two male dancers with pointy cones strapped on their chests like breasts slithered on each side of the bed. The piece culminated in a masturbatory climax that made censors' palms sweat almost everywhere the act played. At the apex of this event, when the music had just ended, Madonna said "God?" and began "Like A Prayer." The stage metamorphosed into a church with a kneeling bench where She, now clad in a black, hooded cape, knelt. The gospel singing like that of the video enlivened the performers as well as the audience as the song progressed.

"Live to Tell" and "Oh Father" were also sung amongst the religious symbols. During the latter, a black priest danced with Madonna in the spirit of the video. Then, following the motif of authority figure, she sang "Papa Don't Preach."

Again the set changed to that of a 1950s musical, and Madonna sang "Sooner or Later" from *Dick Tracy* in the classic style atop a piano. Then she sang her humorous diddy "Hanky Panky," which talked about getting a good spanky. (She wrote "Hanky Panky" in the spirit of Breathless, whom she felt liked to be slapped around.) She performed this number with a dancer dressed as Dick Tracy himself. After that piece Madonna chit-chatted with Dick, who had brought along his own record. When he acted reluctant to play it, Madonna told him that it was okay if

he could not sing. Poking fun at herself, she testified that she couldn't sing either but look how far she's gotten. So they played the old-sounding vinyl record and lip-synched and danced along. The tune was "I'm Following You" from the movie. Then a whole slew of Dick Tracys joined in the dance.

From there, sustaining the comic tone, the scene changed to a beauty parlor, where Madonna, Donna, and Niki sat in monogrammed bathrobes under hairdryers with curlers in their hair. They launched into "Material Girl," during which Madonna shedded the robe to reveal a playful hot pink miniskirt outfit with furry ruffles. At the completion of this number, three smiling mermen joined Madonna on stage for "Cherish."

Before "Into the Groove," Madonna subtly urged the women in her audience that if they really wanted get to know a guy they should ask him to wear a rubber.

After "Vogue," the cast took a bow, but everyone knew that the show was not over yet. Skipping back out in a 1960s-style ruffly polkadot midriff-bearing blouse and hip-hugging, bell-bottom pants, Madonna performed an energetic rendition of "Holiday," incorporating The Bus Stop and The Bump dances along with other psychedelic moves.

She ended the show with "Keep it Together" to which she added some lines from Sly and the Family Stone's "Family Affair." The set was that of a cabaret. She wore yet another outfit for this number, a leather cage over shorts and a bustier, net stockings, fingerless gloves, knee pads, and a derby hat, all black. The whole cast, dancers Luis Camacho, Oliver Crumes, Salim Gauwloos, Jose Gutierez, Kevin Stea, Gabriel Trupin, Carlton Wilborn, and Niki and Donna joined in for this finale, dancing with chairs on which Madonna does some amazing moves. At this song's completion, Madonna was left alone on stage as she continued the phrase "keep it together" unaccompanied and almost in darkness. Eventually, all that remained on the stage was the black derby.

The artistic director of the production was Madonna's brother Christopher Ciccone. The costumes were designed by Jean-Paul Gaultier. Her trainer, Rob Pass, was partly responsible for the star's incredible physical shape. Madonna trained several hours every day, running, cycling, and lifting weights, strengthening her sinewy physique, to endure the gruelling workout of her shows.

Above: Madonna ended every *Ambition* concert with her version of a cabaret. That's what is so intriguing about Madonna—no matter what it is, it's always her interpretation that astounds her audience.

Right: Donning a polkadot blouse is somewhat less flamboyant than Madonna's other show-stopping costumes. But no matter what she wears, she is going to be the center of attention for a long time to come.

in a league of her own

~While the *Blond Ambition* show embodied Madonna the Performer, Madonna the Person was also being documented for all the world to see; filmmaker Alek Keshishian followed Madonna's every move with his camera, and the result was *Truth or Dare*, released in May 1991. Once again Madonna was ubiquitous, appearing in videos on MTV, in the flesh, and on the silver screen.

Truth or Dare, known as *In Bed with Madonna* outside the United States, is narrated by Madonna. Originally, she wanted to film the concert because of its theatrical integrity. Once the show got on the road, however, with the insight of a red-blooded journalist, she realized that the real story was happening backstage. The relationships she was developing with her dancers, whom she began calling her children, were what intrigued her most. The people around her were becoming her family.

Alek Keshishian, a young filmmaker who got the job by a stroke of luck—the filmmaker originally picked backed out at the last minute—shot concert footage in color, but the heart of the documentary, the behind the scenes footage, in 16mm black and white. This technique

Right: Madonna is the Marilyn Monroe of the 1990s. Gentlemen callers try to woo her with their debonair looks. But where are they looking?

emphasized the fact that the Madonna seen in black and white is the real person, not the larger-than-life star. One gets the feeling, however, that all the world's a stage for this woman. It seems that even during private times in this film she is never without an audience. Nor is she ever the audience for anyone else.

When her show rolls into her hometown in Michigan, Madonna, in a robe and shower cap, talks on the phone with her father while slurping a huge bowl of soup in her hotel suite. He asks how many tickets she can get him.

Keshishian sets up a meeting between Madonna and a childhood buddy Moira, who Madonna claims taught her about tampons and sex. Moira denies it all and blames her amnesia on drugs. The meeting is brief and strained, the old friends lives having taken extremely different paths. Madonna seems uncomfortable around the woman, who railroads her into blessing her unborn child, who will be named M.

The backstage meeting with her father and step-mother seems strained as well. It's hard to say if this is a clear view of Madonna's relationship with her parents or if the presence of the camera puts them on edge.

Brother Christopher, who worked as art director of the show, accompanies Madonna to the grave of her mother. In a touching sequence, Madonna talks to and about her mother while laying on her grave with her head on the tombstone. She lays beside her mother's grave, demonstrating the position she will be buried in, and she wonders what her mother looks like now, concluding that she is probably just dust.

Before shows, Madonna leads the group in what starts out as a prayer but ends as a coaching session.

Madonna holds a pajama party at which each dancer gets his own turn to be in bed with her. Then they all climb in and kid around, while there is nonstop R-rated bantering. One of the many subplots depicts Madonna sheltering Oliver, the only heterosexual, from the other dancers.

Above: Madonna, with her entourage of dancers. She insists that everyone stay in strong physical condition. It's a must if the show is to have the intensity she plans on delivering.

Left: Long hours in the recording studio always seems to pay off for the workaholic superstar.

Above: There's always a camera ready to stare at Madonna. She's always ready to stare back.

Right: Madonna with Luke Perry of *Beverly Hills 90210* fame.

Once after a show, Kevin Costner comes backstage to congratulate Madonna and to turn down her invitation to a party afterward. He makes the mistake of calling the show "neat." When he turns to leave, Madonna feigns vomiting and declares that anyone who calls her show "neat" has to go.

While in her hotel suit in Italy, Madonna meets up with her pal Sandra Bernhard. They discuss Madonna's problem with boredom. Sandra asks who Madonna would like to meet. With her head held up in her palms, Madonna replies that she thinks she's met everybody. Madonna's superstar dilemma becomes apparent.

The most talked-about scene of the film has to be the truth or dare game when Madonna fellatiates a bottle. This convincing demonstration is misleading, however, because in real life, Madonna reportedly thinks it is better to receive than give.

The film documents the problem the show had with censorship. The police in Toronto threaten to arrest Madonna after the show if she continues to perform the masturbation act to "Like A Virgin." The stalwart Madonna takes the risk, and the group hurries out of Toronto directly after the show.

When Vatican and certain Catholic communities dissuade the Italian people from buying tickets to see Madonna, she retorts with a convincing speech about freedom of speech and artistic expression. "If you are sure that I am a sinner—then let he who has not sinned cast the first stone," she replies from the Rome airport. She urges those groups to see her show before they judge. "Portraying good and bad, light and dark, joy and sorrow, redemption and salvation. I do not endorse a way of life but describe one, and the audience is left to make its own decisions and judgments. This is what I consider freedom of speech, freedom of expression, and freedom of thought." She calls her show a celebration of love, life, and humanity.

Once at her apartment in New York, Madonna is examined by her throat doctor. The doctor asks if she would prefer to have the exam off-camera, and camera-shy Warren Beatty, whom she was seeing at the

time, explains in an ironical statement that she doesn't want to be seen nor talk off-camera, that for her there is no point existing off-camera. She certainly is in love with the lens. It cannot be denied.

Later Madonna commented on Beatty's lens reluctance, attributing his negativeness to the desire to shroud his life in mystery in the eyes of the public. She says that when the camera was aimed at him he would call the filming ridiculous in hopes that his parts would be edited. This was underestimating Madonna.

In an intimate conversation with her singers, Madonna admits that she is not a superb singer or dancer, but that she has a talent for pushing people's buttons by being provocative and political.

The documentary served as the perfect complement to the concert, because on stage Madonna is super-human, even non-human, whereas behind the scenes she is human. Even so, there is a warmth and vulnerability missing from Madonna the real person. Perhaps achieving what she set out to capture on film is impossible. Once one is aware of an audience, one is automatically a performer.

The film opened in May 1991. It was screened in a non-competitive category at the Cannes Film Festival that same month. In a weird coincidence, Sean Penn's latest film was also in the festival, and he was there with his new wife Robin Wright and their infant. Madonna got more attention and raised more excitement than anyone had seen at that festival since the reign of old-fashioned film stars. *Truth or Dare* was later released on video, selling for almost $100.

Many critics thought that making such a personal, revealing documentary on the private life of Madonna would be a suicidal career move. It would reveal her vulnerable, real side and shatter the illusion. But Madonna's career has done nothing but strengthen as a result.

Madonna released *The Immaculate Collection* in 1990, a compilation album which consisted of remixes of previously released singles as well as

Above: Madonna leading her performers in a group prayer. This is a ritual before every concert.

Left: Just another night on the town—never going unnoticed, never wearing a frown.

two new pieces, "Rescue Me" and "Justify My Love." And *The Immaculate Collection* video contains all the great Madonna videos from "Borderline" to "Vogue."

The video for "Justify My Love" was so sizzlingly sexual that MTV declined to air it. Controversy had everyone stirring in reaction to the homosexual, voyeuristic, androgynous, and nude images in the video. Madonna was quick to point out the twisted morays of television and film, which portray people killing and getting killed everyday but shudder at the thought of two women kissing or two men snuggling, considering that too obscene. (This was not the first time that Madonna had spoken out about the overabundance of violence on TV and in films. She has also criticized parents' irresponsibility for allowing their children to watch violent shows.)

Filming for this video was done on the sixth floor of the Royal Monceau Hotel in Paris. It took three days and was completed in utter secrecy. The song, a whimsical monologue of sexual fantasy, was written by Ingrid Chavez and Lenny Kravitz, and the video was directed by Jean-Baptiste Mondino.

In it, Madonna's character, dressed in sexy black lingerie, tells her fantasies to real-life boyfriend, Tony Ward. Among images of people of various sexual orientations are glimpses of her making love first with a woman, androgynous model Amanda Cazalet, and then with Ward. The video shows homosexuality, voyeurism, cross-dressing,

multiple partners, and sadomasochism. At the end of the sizzling five-minute video appear the words, "Poor is the man whose pleasures depend on the permission of another." Madonna has since explained her view that everyone has a bisexual nature. She says that this video represents the interior of a person's mind.

Undaunted by MTV's censorship, Madonna marketed the video, selling five times more copies than the best selling videos. Many other television networks and programs saw the opportunity to raise the ratings by airing the video, including CNN, Fox, Saturday Night Live, Entertainment Tonight, and Nightline, which also interviewed Madonna. When the show's host pointed out the fact that the ban by MTV was actually working to benefit Madonna, she replied with a smile, "Yeah, so lucky me." Madonna drew the line for what she considers acceptable at violence, humiliation, and degradation.

Also in 1990, on the MTV awards in September, Madonna and her cast performed a Restoration version of "Vogue," nominated for three awards, complete with fops, rakes and a great deal of fan-breaking. Madonna stole the show in her powdered wig and four-foot-wide pannier skirt.

MTV also aired a public announcement made by Madonna, rapping while wrapped in the American flag, for MTV's "Rock the Vote." Ironically Madonna herself didn't vote in that election.

At this point Madonna was making $39 million gross, according to *Forbes* magazine. But what really set Madonna apart from other multi-million dollar entertainers was the fact that she ran her own affairs. The woman knows business.

The November 1991 issue of *Architectural Digest* featured Madonna's Manhattan apartment as decorated by her brother Christopher. The seven and one-half rooms contain early French deco furniture and art by the likes of Picasso, Dali, Ray, and of course Kahlo, Madonna's idol. Madonna also has her own gym and an old-fashioned kitchen for her friends to cook in, since she doesn't.

In 1991 Madonna appeared in Woody Allen's film *Shadows and Fog* with other esteemed actors Mia Farrow, John Malkovich, Lily Tomlin, Kathy Bates, and Jodie Foster. In it she plays a 1920s circus performer. Although her role is small, more like a cameo appearance, Madonna is surrounded by the best actors in the profession. Her decision to accept such a role, in which she is just one of an ensemble instead of the star, was a wise and strategic one, since she wishes to be considered a serious actor.

The same is true for her role in *A League of Their Own*, starring Geena Davis and Tom Hanks, which opened in July 1992. This movie is about the All-American Girl's Professional Baseball League in 1943. There was some serious ball-playing done for this film. Madonna trained with a real baseball coach, and she took some hits during practice, including one that gave her a shiner.

Madonna plays the gum-chewing, wise-cracking center-fielder May, the "ball player with an attitude." May,

Above: In *A League Of Their Own* (1992) Madonna co-starred as a ballplayer who always scored high with men.

Right: In 1991 she had a cameo role in Woody Allen's film *Shadows and Fog*. She played a circus performer and was surrounded by stars. Madonna's doing something right to be acting alongside some of the biggest names in the movie business.

a.k.a. All The Way May, and her sidekick Dolores, played by Rosie O'Donnell, provide the comic relief to an otherwise tear-jerking sentimental story. In one particularly funny scene, Dolores and some other ball players are waiting outside the confessional in a Catholic church while May is inside with a priest, who keeps dropping his bible, shocked at her confessions. She steps out of the booth looking cherubic, kneels, crosses herself, winks at a young boy, and exits, leaving the others dumbfounded with their jaws hanging, including the priest.

Madonna not only plays baseball well, she commands everyone's attention with her 1940s-style jitterbugging that clears the dance floor. And, of course, Madonna wrote and performed the theme song, "This Used to be My Playground."

The significance of Madonna's participation in this movie is that it is woman-affirming. The film reveals the sexist views that women endured in the 1940s. Madonna's character is strong, which is a significant criterion for her when she chooses a role.

In 1992, Madonna signed a $60 million deal with Time-Warner, Inc. which included her own recording, music and book publishing, television and film, and merchandising company, Maverick. In October 1992, Maverick released both the music video, *Erotica*, and Madonna's album of the same name. In the video, Madonna reinvents herself as the masked dominatrix, urging us to "Give it up, do as I say," in a series of sexually explicit clips with sadomasochistic and homoerotic messages. Keeping with the theme of *Erotica,* her company's first publishing venture, *Sex,* is a photographic romp with Dita, a sexual adventuress played by none other than Madonna herself.

In her next film, *Body of Evidence* (1992), Madonna plays a woman enthralled by sadomasochism. Her character attempts to murder her lawyer, played by Willem Dafoe, by thrilling him sexually to the point of heart attack.

Though it cannot be denied that the roles Madonna has most success in are ones in which she is depicted as a seductress, Madonna criticizes the sexist double standard, the fact that her overt sexuality makes people think she is promiscuous when they think nothing of the same image of a male star. Similarly, she was initially compared with Cyndi Lauper, as if there was only room for one female pop singer when there can never be too many male ones.

There is a stark contrast between Madonna and other extremely culturally pervasive and wealthy stars. Madonna considers herself a role-model for her young fans, and she accepts and takes seriously that responsibility. She urges people through her music and her star persona to be themselves, to keep a positive outlook on life, and to love themselves, and she offers them tools of empowerment. Madonna also knows that she stands for the sex goddess image in the minds of her fans.

Below: Batting a thousand isn't anything new to Madonna. Her hit songs have brought the big-league star around the bases and then some.

Left: Madonna and Tom Hanks talking it up in *A League Of Their Own.*

She is especially appealing to and appreciated by women, representing everything women are taught not to be by their mothers and grandmothers. Her music is affirming and encouraging, promoting dignity, self-respect, and sexual expression. Another aspect to the feminist paradox is Madonna's apparent femininity. She thinks that the pitfall of the women's movement is that women wanted to be like men.

As for the future, she is planning to produce and star in films on dancer/choreographer Martha Graham and artist Frida Kahlo, her idols. Then there is the age-old possibility of playing Eva Peron in a film about the Argentinean first lady. She also plans to act in movies with Demi Moore and Uma Thurman.

Now Madonna is on a different kind of mission. She is frequenting the Delphian oracle seeking knowledge of the self. She is also sinking

Above and right. You would think with all the flashbulbs that have gone off in Madonna's face, it would grow a little tiresome. If it has, she never makes it look that way.

herself deeper into the environment of serious art. Madonna's favorite artists are Frida Kahlo and Georgia O'Keeffe, two powerful women. One can understand the attraction. When she gets older, she wants to be a patron of the arts like Peggy Guggenheim. With ambitions like these, Madonna is sure to remain one in a million.

discography

Madonna (1983)

Like A Virgin (1984)

True Blue (1986)

You Can Dance (1987)

Like A Prayer (1989)

I'm Breathless (1990)

The Immaculate Collection (1990)

Erotica (1992)

films

Vision Quest (1985)

Desperately Seeking Susan (1985)

Shanghai Surprise (1986)

Who's That Girl? (1987)

Bloodhounds of Broadway (1989)

Dick Tracy (1990)

Truth or Dare (1991)

A League of Their Own (1992)

Body of Evidence (1992)

tours

Virgin Tour (1985)

Who's That Girl Tour (1987)

Blond Ambition Tour (1990)

plays

Speed-the-Plow (1988)

books

Sex (1992)

index

Left: James Cagney and James Dean couldn't have done it much better than this. Madonna's a rebel with a cause and a definite contender for pop artists to come.

Page 72: One thing's for sure. All the world's an audience for the queen of music, as she is the stage.